Finding
BIG MO

Finding
BIG MO

DREW Y. SANDERS

Dedicated to
My Mom and Dad, and
to Ray "Foot" Mednis

TABLE OF CONTENTS

CHAPTER ONE

Paired With A Monster

Thomas Barr stood on the first tee of the Pebble Beach Golf Links in a cold sweat. He was paired in the final group of the United States Open Championship with seven-time champion, Cyrus Steele. The announcer had been listing Cy's past accomplishments for what felt like an hour. Tom's bio had been short and barely sweet: "Please welcome Thomas Barr, competing in his first U.S. Open Championship and the winner of the 2009 Merced County Open." The smattering of applause he had received was mostly from his college buddies, who had rolled in for the weekend when he managed to make the cut by a few shots. They stuck around when he caught fire on Saturday with a front-nine 30 and then held on to shoot 66 and be the overnight leader by two over Steele.

Finishing early on Saturday and talking with the press about his blistering start had been the last time anything seemed to go right for Tom. As it stood now, he didn't even think he was going to be able to take the club back, let alone breathe, and when he did breathe the smell of whiskey coming off his caddy's breath was enough to knock him over.

The fact that he had a new caddy added another layer of stress to the biggest round of his life. How had his faithful sidekick, Billy, picked last night as the first time in his life to try oysters at one of those tourist traps in Monterey? The menu's idea of "fresh" and Billy's stomach hadn't jived, and at present he was in a hospital bed with his hand on the remote control.

The new guy, whom Tom had found sleeping in the caddy yard that morning, came with only a nickname: The Foot. Razor thin and extremely tall, Foot was a bit of a legend at Pebble Beach. When awake and somewhat sober, he had been on the bag for more wins than any other caddy in course history. Now well past his prime, he hadn't scored a bag for the Open because he was only good for one round a week. The Open was a week-long grind, including practice and competitive rounds. Foot also carried another distinction that led most people to leave him alone: he spoke in a weird code that worked wonders with some people. For most tour players, though, he made no sense. He was always talking about his friend "Mo" and those players who stumbled, having fallen victim to the "Beast."

The combination of his age, odor, and communication style led to his availability that Sunday morning when Tom finally came to grips with the fact that Billy wasn't going to make it to the course. The caddy master assured Tom that Foot was actually ready to go. "He was once the best there was and if you catch his vibe on how to dance with Pebble on a day like today, he just might be the best thing that ever happened to you."

The Foot had looked him over, smiled slightly, and slowly picked himself up off the bench. Now five hours later, with 30,000 people in attendance and several million TV viewers watching from around the world, it was Tom's turn to play away.

His two-iron felt like a feather in his hand and feeling the clubhead was nearly impossible. Tom's swing was a little quick and shorter than normal and he caught the ball a groove low and towards the heel. This created a low screaming left to right ball flight that felt like he had put his finger in an electrical outlet. Somehow the ball found the fairway.

The small army of players, caddies, camera crews, standard bearers and tournament officials that makes up the final group in a major championship took off towards their tee shots. Tom figured that his opponent wasn't going to speak to him the entire round, short of a grunt about who was away or if a ball mark could be fixed on the green. This could have been a challenge, as Tom was someone who liked to talk with Billy during the round. He wasn't sure what to ask Foot, so he was quite surprised when the caddy offered first.

"How did the press conference go yesterday?"

It was a very direct question, and Tom didn't know why Foot was asking.

"Fine, I guess. Most of them didn't know anything about me."

"What did they ask you?" Foot asked.

"Where I am from, who my teacher is, do I have family in town?"

"What else?" he replied.

"I don't know. Do I like the golf course? Why am I playing well?"

"Did they ask you if you are going to win today?" Foot looked at Tom with a glare in his eye.

They were almost at his ball and he was going to be the first to play. Tom was beginning to wonder if he should pull one of his knucklehead buddies out of the crowd, so he could think about playing golf versus a game of Twenty Questions with his rather odoriferous and now deep-thinking caddy. He decided against that notion and looked at Foot.

"Yes they did, and I told them I really liked the golf course, was ready to play my best, and have always been up for great challenges. Today is surely going to be one of those."

Foot looked at him for several seconds then said, "Good. That should keep the Beast of Expectation in his place. He likes to hang out in the trees on the right side of this hole and derail players who are over confident."

Having arrived at his ball, Tom went to his back left pocket for his yardage book. Suddenly a series of crisp and clear data points came out of Foot's mouth followed by a charge: "You've got 132 front, 149 hole. There is a ridge running up the middle that you have to aim at and a slight ocean breeze that can hold up a fade that starts too far left. With the hole cut against that right bunker, it's the perfect nine-iron to hit 143 yards. Swing with confidence and freedom."

He said all this while pulling the bag down off his shoulder and situating it in an angle towards Tom, which would allow him to pull the club himself.

Tom's mouth was agape. His mind had been racing. A beast? Had he heard that right—there was a beast in the trees on the right? Who talks about a beast on the first hole of the U.S. Open?

The yardage talk, however, had him locked in right away and he grabbed the nine-iron. Within seconds, he had his ball flying directly towards the back middle of the green where it took one hop to the right and then stopped 15 feet beneath the hole. The crowd clapped with enthusiasm as the ball came to rest, and Tom found his putter in his hands and his nine-iron back in the bag, freshly wiped clean by Foot.

Cy had striped a low trajectory three-iron off the tee with a hold-off fade that was his trademark shot. He breathed out slowly after hitting the shot. The crowd took in their own collective breath with a gasp as the ball shot past them with a purpose seldom seen. His 118-yard gap wedge had hit inches away from where Tom's had landed, but his ball kicked left, away from the hole, and he had an awkward 18-footer with close to six feet of break. Most of the crowd rejoiced in his shot, but Cy sneered at his misfortune and took the chance to ramp up the engine of negativity that he used as his personal mechanism for greatness. Very few people knew that what went along with Cy's trophies was a trophy case full of hate as well. He used this to chew up golf courses and devour competitors who came in his path. He seldom spoke to them, nor did he need to as his aura and body language coupled with his game usually did the trick. For Cy golf was a game of control, and the easiest way to get control and the easiest way to get others out of control was to open up a huge jar of hate and fear. Let the tension fill the air until his competitors couldn't breathe.

Cy figured that the few shots he had to make up on this no-name rookie should be taken care of by the sixth tee, and after that it would be just Cy and the course he knew like the back of his hand. The two players reached the treacherous green and both managed pars, with Cy having to spend much more time and energy than Tom due to where his ball had ended up.

Both players' drives landed in the fairway on the tough second hole and again, Tom found Foot to be quite an interesting conversationalist.

"What's the best way to get from Merced to Los Angeles?" he asked first.

"How long have you had these irons?" Foot asked later. "They look to fit you perfectly."

"Tell me about the best four-iron you ever hit," he prompted Tom when they approached the ball.

As Tom was recalling a four-iron over water to a tucked flag he had hit in Texas last fall, they got to the ball and once again Foot went from conversationalist to data computer with a punch line.

"You've got 187 front, 203 hole with 8 yards of uphill and a half club of hurting wind coming out of the right. The first bounce on this green or short is firm, but then it slows quickly. The lie is perfect so let's hit it with gusto and see what the gods have in store for us."

Again the bag was tilted perfectly so that the four-iron was there for Tom to grab and swing with freedom. The lie was fast and perfect, and as the club hit the ball the sound was that of a vacuum of space and matter. Tom stuck his finish, and with solid contact and good balance the grace of a long iron unfolded in front of them and the world. Precisely 191 yards later the ball landed with some teeth, bounced up, and then settled twelve feet short of the hole. The crowd had followed the ball the entire time and with pent up angst let out a roar of approval that lasted a bit longer than Cy thought was appropriate.

Cy's ball had found the fairway, but the lie was average. The ensuing five-iron was more of an act of brute force than grace and its low trajectory caused it to land well short and end up five feet in front of the green. He again released his most exasperated and disgusted reaction to the shot, and his glare now seemed to flow in Tom's direction.

Who was this kid? And, more importantly, who was this beatnik caddy and what were they talking about?

Tom and Foot were now engaged in a different dialogue as Tom asked Foot a question.

"So who is this beast that hangs out on the first hole?" Foot gave Tom a sideways glance and brought his finger up to his lips. "Careful! The Beast of Expectation lives under the bridge just off the fourth tee and circles the first five holes claiming his victims. We are the last group, so the chances of him hearing us are high. Keep your voice down."

"Okay," Tom said and lowered his voice.

"Who is he?" Foot asked, repeating Tom's question. "Pebble Beach is a special place with many rounds of golf in the books since Jack Neville and Robert Hunter laid out the course in 1919. Over the years it has collected a series of spirits, some good and some bad. My job as your caddy is to help you avoid the beasts and to see if we can get Big Mo to come hang out with us for a while."

Tom had his putter in his hand and they were reaching the green when they were met with a round of applause, most of it for Tom.

"We will pick this up on the next hole," Foot said.

"Your putt is left center with no trick speeds, pick a small spot on the back of the cup and take some dirt off the back of the cup with this one for me."

Tom and Foot made their way to the back right of the green as Cy prepared his chip shot. No one moved when Cy was about to play. He was a fantastic champion but required absolute silence. He played a brilliant chip shot that landed squarely, didn't check too much, and released towards the hole. As it rolled it seemed destined for the cup and the crowd started to rumble in anticipation. Having been online for over 40 feet, it lost a bit of its purpose and tailed off at the last for a tap-in par. The easily pleased crowd applauded vigorously and all looked to Cy for a tip of the cap or a smile. None was found. Cy ripped off his glove and demonstrated with his hand how unjustly the ball had broken off at the last. He had been robbed! None of this was for the crowd, and Foot knew it. It was an act to ensnare his player, to suck Tom into Cy's trap of misery. Foot knew that no one in the world played better golf while miserable than Cy.

Foot leaned into Tom a bit as all eyes watched Cy's act.

"Hey Tom," whispered Foot.

"Yes," Tom replied.

"Take some paint off the back of that cup for me, will yah? I want to see if we can't wake up old Mo with a roar from that crowd."

Tom had been in touch with the seaside poa annua greens all week and with the added confidence of Foot's read stepped up and drilled the ball solidly into the center of the cup for a birdie three. The noise from the crowd sent sound waves all across the third, fourth, sixteenth and seventeenth holes, some of it even reaching the eighteenth tee. Deep inside one of the caves that sit beneath that final tee, Big Mo started to wake from a nap.

CHAPTER 2

Finding Mo

"Mo" is short for Momentum. In scientific terms it is easily understood. Mass times velocity, a simple binary equation. But in terms of personal performance, Mo is the flightiest of creatures, here one minute and gone the next. In golf, Mo is something the great ones have often talked about. But for most golfers it only lasts a few shots or holes, and then with one bad shot seems to disappear.

In the final round of this U.S. Open at Pebble Beach almost nobody had any Mo, as the hole locations were brutal and the course had been starved of water. Like always, the USGA had it playing firm and fast. Mo had been out early to see if anyone was going to need his services, but most golfers were so worn down from the week that he had gone back to his home and dozed off. The faint roar that awoke him seemed to have potential and so he adjusted his position to the front of his cave and watched the waves roll in.

Both players played safely on three, laying back to a distance where they could impart some spin into the front-to-back pitched and hardening third green. This time Cy opened play and he hit a high arching gap wedge that landed just over the right bunker. The ball took a six-foot high hop and then as if an Indy car was backing up at full throttle, the ball screeched to a stop a mere four feet to the right of the hole. The thousands of fans along both sides of the fairway and those around the green cheered the great champion's effort. Cy raised an acknowledging hand while toeing in a divot with the other. He appeared more concerned with the divot than the applause, but he knew by acknowledging the crowd he would spur them on and that should have an impact on his young challenger.

Foot knew that trying to match the shot by Cy would only bring in the trouble of the bunker or the slope that caused balls to rocket across the green into the five-inch rough that surrounded the diminutive par-four. Tom's ball was further to the right, which changed how the ball would react on the green. With this in mind, Foot steered Tom's focus away from the flag after outlining the facts of the shot.

"You've got 89 front, 102 hole. Your angle of attack is more to the right than Cy's, so we won't be able to stop the ball as easily. When we throw it past the hole, the green is flatter, plus it will allow you to hit a full shot. The slight hurting breeze should help the spin, but let's throw it 103 and fifteen feet to the left."

Tom knew the lie was hanging a bit and also above his feet. He pulled his 54-degree wedge from the bag, went through his routine and let it go. His ball didn't fly as high as Cy's. It didn't have as much grab to it, but it did land on one of the flatter parts of the green. The ball released ten feet and he had a flattish 22-foot putt.

The third green stands above its surroundings, and as the two players walked to their balls they appeared like larger-than-life heroes to the adoring golf fans milling around the green. Tom's putt had the distance of 22 feet to Cy's four, but Tom's was all uphill and Cy's was a cliff hanger that would either go in or easily scoot five feet by if it missed. While preparing to play, Foot could feel Cy's frustration that his ball hadn't kicked down below the hole. His continued state of despair and disgust was highly contagious; he was literally oozing misery and he started to make an effort to get closer to Tom. Foot recognized his tactic and stumbled in Cy's direction to ward him off. It did the trick. Foot righted himself and then leaned into Tom's ear and said: "We've caught a break here. I have seen this putt made time and time again. Most think it's a left-to-right putt and that the back of the green dominates the break, but actually at the hole it goes left because of the hill coming off the bunker. Put it a ball out on the right and let it go."

Tom in his connected state of listening to everything Foot said got set over the ball and played it out on the right. Everyone watched as the ball broke right at first and then in the last six feet turned left and fell into the cup on its last roll. Bedlam ensued as not only was the crowd on three watching, but the grandstand at the seventeenth tee also afforded a view of the action. The rookie was on fire again and the champ was now in the pressure box with a tricky four-footer to stay within three shots of the lead.

Foot winked at Tom as the two joined up on the front of the green to avoid being in Cy's line of sight for his putt. Tom looked back with a big smile and said, "Billy and I would have never seen that second break."

All of the attention around Tom's start had Cy focused. A cauldron of pressure was his playground. He stalked the putt from all sides and then calmly struck it home to stay three back. He didn't flinch as the sound of the crowd reverberated throughout the seaside links; he just moved in stride to the next tee. He did this dance of pressure putting for a living and no rookie was going to shake him.

Back under the eighteenth tee, Mo had perked up at the first roar and was out of his cave by the second one. He looked to see who might need his help after all.

Tom and Cy made their way through holes four and five in par and the rookie's lead remained three shots. Tom had passed the first test with his ability to be humble in his approach to the day. He had adapted to his inability to feel the clubhead at first and his tension free swings had allowed him to attract Mo to his side. He had sidestepped the Beast of Expectation, which allowed him to get into his round and actually extend his lead. Tom didn't realize that along with giving him great insight to the course, Foot was playing a key role in keeping him out of Cy's misery trap. The final pairing made their way up to the sixth tee, and the first stanza of the final round came to a close.

Tom had the honor and launched his best drive of the day far down the right side of the fairway. His ball was at the base of the hill that makes up the beginning of Arrowhead Point which hosts the sixth green, seventh hole, and eighth tee.

Cy pulled his tee shot to the left and just missed going into the enormous fairway bunker that frames the short but exciting par-five. His ball was still in the intermediate rough, and from the tee it wasn't clear what type of lie he had drawn. His lie would dictate how he played the hole. Cy ignored the break he had received and rather let out a loud *"Cy"* so that he could share his displeasure with his surroundings, partially hoping they would think, *Gosh, if he is this good while missing every shot, he will be unstoppable when he starts squaring it up.*

Foot was having none of Cy's act and started pep-
pering Tom with more stories about the spirits
that lived around Pebble Beach.

"Yep, for a time after they took out the old tree
on eighteen green, no one could eagle the hole.
Every time a player was on in two shots, their
putt would go off line for no reason. We figured
it was the roots of the old tree moving around
under the green as a way to get revenge."

Tom thought that sounded a bit hokey, but for
sure Foot had been right about getting Mo to
show up. Tom was crushing the ball off the tee,
hitting his spots with the irons and rolling it very
well on the greens. If there was a zone, he was in
it! He said as much to Foot as they got to the ball
on six. "You know Foot, if I keep this up, I could
be in the Masters next year."

Foot almost fell over the bag on the spot and
looked as if someone had kept him from his Jim
Beam for a week. "What on earth are you trying
to do, Tom?" was his remark. "Don't you know
that the Write Your Own Headlines Beast lives
right over there in a cave on Stillwater Cove? He

lives down there because lots of people get off to fast starts and start flapping their gums about how they might have their best round ever. He may not catch them on six or seven, but typically around eight, nine and ten he has laid waste to their scores. Let's hope he wasn't around to hear that and get back to the shot at hand."

Then he reset Tom's mind by delivering the figures. "You've got 204 front, 230 hole. The green is made up of four parts, with a spine in the middle that is very unforgiving. The apron is tightly mowed and hasn't been watered in days. Your lie is cross grain and our angle dictates as lofted a club as possible to get up on top of the hill." Foot tilted the clubs towards Tom, who pulled a three-iron and got ready to play. Foot shook the clubs a bit after Tom pulled the iron but stood to the side knowing a confused golfer is a poor one and awaited the result.

The result was that Tom was still thinking about the Masters and who he might send his tickets to. The three-iron, when well struck, was plenty of club and actually may have been too much stick. The real problem was that if he missed it at all, the loft on the club might not be enough to climb the hill, and with his angle he would be crossing the hazard most of the way.

Miss it he did by hitting it on the toe and a touch fat. The ball was a dying quail from the moment it hit its apex and the ball barely crossed the hazard before kicking to the right and going off the cliff. If the ball had not cleared the hazard, they would have been dropping at the base of the hill again and headed for a big number.

Cy had played earlier and was on the green in two shots with an eagle putt. He picked up his step as Tom's ball fell to its demise. Tom shoulders sank forward and his thoughts got very narrow. Tension filled his body.

"Did it cross the hazard, Foot? What is that marshal signaling? Where do I drop it?"

Foot, for his part, was on the move; he knew what to do and had seen the Beast of Headlines strike before. Worse yet, Tom would think that Big Mo was gone for good and with holes eight to ten coming up, it would take some real skill to share with Tom that Mo sticks around after a bad swing or hole but only to see if you keep your positive attitude. Most people don't and that is when he leaves.

The fact that Tom's ball had carried the hazard and landed on the course was a huge break. Foot made a beeline for that spot to get the numbers in place and help Tom stay in the game. He would be hitting his fourth shot from 120 yards on a par-five, while Cy had a putt for three. They could be even at the end of the hole; most likely the lead would be down to one shot.

Tom reached his drop spot several minutes after Foot who had the new ball out and was armed with the relevant info and his lesson.

"It's 102 front, 124 hole, with a half-club hurting wind from the right. Your lie could be a jumper from the look of the grass. Let's fly it 112 and have it release to the hole. Look for the good here."

Tom's action through the ball lacked commitment; he was still shaking off the last shot and the lie ended up helping him. Had the ball been in the fairway the marginal contact would have sent the ball careening across the green. However, in the light rough the ball climbed up the club face, arched higher than normal, and bounded towards the hole. Fifteen feet for par.

Eight minutes later, they walked off the green having both two-putted. Cy met Tom's bogey with an easy birdie. As Foot had anticipated, the lead was cut to one.

Steele had the honor on seven, and it sure looked like Big Mo had left Tom's camp and shifted his attention to Cy.

Between the short distance of the sixth green and the seventh tee, Foot pulled Tom aside. "Do you remember on one when you said you liked challenges?" Food asked. "Did you really mean it?"

Tom looked right back at him and said, "You know, Foot, my mom always said I was like a cork. You could push me down in one spot and I would come up some place else. I guess I always have liked a challenge."

"Good," Foot said, "because the next eight holes are some of the most challenging in golf. If we stick together, I bet you we can keep Big Mo going in our direction. What do you say we hit a quality shot here?"

"You're on!" said Tom

CHAPTER 3

Poison Darts

They caught up to the group on the tee. Big Mo noticed that Tom had kept his positive attitude. He knew Cy's need for him was minimal. Steele never shared any of his glory with others and while Mo had to be there with him when he was hot, they never became close because Cy always hogged the spotlight after a win. Not once in 65 wins had Cy shared the credit with Mo or anyone else.

Holes seven and eight were played with hard fought pars and both players bogeyed the difficult ninth. Tom had played the nine holes in even par and Cy had made up one shot by playing them in one-under. Tom stuck to his routine of enjoying the challenge of each shot and staying in the present. He and Foot had a good rapport built up, and Tom had stopped looking at his yardage book to double check the numbers after the fourth hole. He was walking up to his ball, visualizing its flight, and then picking a club and executing that vision with freedom.

Better still was the fact that for nine holes Tom had felt as if he was playing by himself, because Foot had kept him engaged in conversation. He had barely noticed Cy's antics and efforts to bring the group into the misery trap. Walking to the tenth tee, Cy could see that the kid had game. He decided to start turning up the heat a bit to tilt the table in his direction as soon as possible. Cy had the honor and it turned out they were forced to wait on the long par-four that has cliffs leading to the Carmel Beach on the right. Cy noticed that Foot had left for the restroom, so he took the opportunity to speak with Tom.

"You know Tom," Cy said, "I have never surfed up here in Nor Cal. I am too afraid of the great white sharks that eat the seals. A surfer in a wetsuit looks like big seal to those monsters. Can you believe anyone would go out there in those conditions?"

Tom, stunned that Cy was actually addressing him, responded like a school boy answering a teacher's question. "Gosh, I haven't looked out there that much. I've just been trying to focus on each shot. I guess that water is pretty close. Those guys are nuts."

Cy smiled and turned to his tee shot just as Foot came back to the group. Foot could tell something was different about Tom but couldn't place it. Cy had skillfully placed a poison dart of distraction and hazard in Tom's subconscious. Steele needed to get the kid off his game and get him worried and start feeling the moment.

Cy's ball was teed down and he hit a low trajectory bullet that peeled left to right off the left fairway bunker. The bunker sat atop the steeply slopped fairway that ran down to the cliffs on the right. The ball landed hot and pitched forward some 60 yards. Cy was looking at maybe 130 in, with a great angle to the back left flag.

Tom teed his ball just as low and had the same intent as Cy, but his distracted mind pulled the ball away from the ocean and it actually landed left of the bunkers in the deep rough.

Tom played the entire hole out of position and had to make a six-foot putt for bogey, while Cy played a knockdown nine-iron to twelve feet and made the putt for birdie. Cy's plan had worked; he had riled the kid. It had taken five holes longer than he had planned, but Steele had a one-shot lead with eight holes to play and the tee was his.

Tom and Foot chatted as they walked off the eleventh tee, with Cy leading the charge up the hill.

"You know he talked to me on the tenth tee while you were away?" Tom said. "He actually is a pretty nice guy, we talked about surfing."

"Surfing? You talked about surfing?" Foot responded. "Do you think after 65 victories and with nine holes to play that Cy decided now was the time to start being your new best friend? Let me guess: he got you to look at the hazard so you would play away from it and get yourself out of position for a back left flag!"

Tom realized his mistake. "Well, I didn't think about it that way. I thought he liked how I was playing and decided to shoot the breeze while we waited."

"Tom," Foot said. "Cy Steele doesn't 'shoot the breeze' with anybody, let alone a tour rookie who stands between him and an eighth U.S. Open Title.

Let's tighten up the focus a bit here and see if we can't get past the final Beast and get Big Mo to swing to our side when we need it."

The two were now in agreement and returned to their comfortable dialogue patterns. Foot started talking about the spirit of Bing Crosby that hung out in the oak trees to the right of the twelfth green. Bing had kept a house on the thirteenth hole for years, but his spirit liked the action at twelve. Caddies told of being able to hear the famous crooner's voice as they went from twelfth green to the thirteenth fairway during their loops.

Tom righted the ship on holes eleven and twelve and was matched by Steele with pars. He caught his drive a little on the heel on thirteen while Cy had hit a hammer draw far up the left side. The hole was cut back left, and the two players would have completely different yardages and angles to one of the most severely right-to-left pitched greens on the course. Any ball that found the right side of the green would inevitably go left and quite often would go back towards the front. The area around the flag was a plateau. Long was above the hole and left fell down a steep decline—both dead. Tom was well back, in mid-iron range. Cy was directly in line with flag on the left side of the fairway and 120 yards out.

Foot stood on the tee with Tom. There were a few more things to chat about and he hung back with his charge to let Cy lead the way down the fairway. Tom by now was attached at the hip to Foot. He went into his bag to get a banana. The two would be first to play, but the pace of play was such that they would have plenty of time to get to their ball and be in position.

Tom and Foot chatted about a variety of subjects on the way to the ball. They had a good flow going and their routine had become almost ironclad. They would jump from discussion about challenges and adventures in the long intervals walking from the tee to the ball. Then when it was time to focus, Foot would present the data and an action-oriented charge. Tom was able to get into a rhythm and his body felt in total sync with his clubs. Every sense in his body was back to functioning at a very high level. He felt the pitch in the ground with his feet and the wind on his cheek; his eyes noticed the trees moving, gauging the wind in correlation with what he felt at eye level. As he came into his shots, he could actually see with his mind the trajectory of the ball in flight and picture how the ball would land and release.

On any other course, he might have been on a birdie barrage, but in the final round of the Open his best shots were setting up twelve- to twenty-foot putts. Pebble Beach's heavily sloped and very small greens demanded precision.

Tom had kept Mo on his side by being open for challenges, practicing his routine, and staying in the present. Tom had also survived several attacks from Cy and the Beast of Writing Your Own Headlines. Foot had helped him let those obstacles present themselves and then move past them as quickly as possible. "No one gets to compete in a vacuum, Tom. Someone, somebody, or something is going to be along with you as you seek your best performance. In fact, without challenges or challengers you wouldn't know what your best was. You have to accept the obstacle, be flexible enough to adapt, and then have a flush button to get it out of your mental system as efficiently as possible."

"We are all learning our way to cultivate our own personal momentum, and the great ones end up becoming highly contagious mentors and teachers. They exist in every sport and profession and they are rewarded with great relationships with others wherever they go. They may not end up with the most trophies, but they claim their share and you will notice the freedom with which they move and the peace with which they compete."

They got to their ball, and it appeared someone else had hit a weak fade. Tom's ball was in the middle of a shallow and long divot. The TV cameras and the announcers had noticed it right away. By the time Tom and Foot had made it to the ball, the world was watching to see how the rookie would react to this tremendously bad break.

Foot, always looking a little further into the future than Tom, had a wry smile on his face. This would be a great test to see where Tom was emotionally. He was also curious how high Tom could reach as a competitor on this world stage.

CHAPTER 4

Me vs. The Beasts

To Foot this was the break of a lifetime in their favor, but he wasn't sure Tom would have the ability to process the challenge in enough time for them to take advantage of it.

"A divot? Am I in a divot, Foot? What are the chances that I am in a divot in a fairway that is 24 by 60 yards long? On top of that, I heeled it! Every divot should be up near where Cy's ball finished."

"Yep." Foot replied. "And I think this could really work in our favor," said the lanky caddie.

Tom looked at him funny and said, "How so?"

"Well…" Foot launched into his data dump. "Keep your ears on and trust me. You've got 164 front, 186 hole. The back left plateau starts at 176. With a normal lie you would have to maneuver a low swing speed shot to land before 176 and have it release up the slope. That is a tall order, which means we would most likely be taking our medicine and playing to the front of the green. Cy is up there with a one-shot lead just itching to throw a dart in close and get the crowd revved up. Being two shots down with five to Cy play might be a tall order. Here's the good news. That divot you're in will make the ball come out low and with less spin, so when you land it at 170 it should release up to the plateau. Can you see it?"

Tom squinted a bit and the announcers chuckled like he was losing his eyesight. "The air is pretty thin when you're trying to win an Open title," one anchor offered.

"Yeah, I can see it," Tom said, "and this divot is just the right size for a gripped down six-iron."

"Great," Foot said, "let's stick the landing and play a shot."

The TV camera caught the caddy tilting the bag in Tom's direction so that he could pull his club. The on-course reporter who had seen the lie picked up Tom's confidence and said, "You know this kid knows what he wants to do with this shot, and if I had to lay odds right now I would say he is going to pull something off."

Tom's six-iron came into the divot and kicked through with speed. The ball compressed a groove low and he was in balance as he held his finish on the slightly up hill terrain.

Foot heard the contact, saw the balance in Tom's finish and picked up the trajectory of the searing white sphere. He started reaching for the putter. The ball landed at 168, took a quick kick forward and then lost its speed into the hill and crested the subtle ledge. It came to rest thirteen feet below and to the left of the hole.

The TV announcers were apoplectic with praise for the artistry, the fans in attendance were euphoric in their applause, and 40 yards up Cy was seeing red!

"How can that rookie be pulling this off? He won't go away, doesn't he know this is the Open and this is my turf. I make the rules, I am in control, and he needs to be taught a lesson."

Cy pulled his gap wedge out of his bag and prepared to hit a full nuke high spinner with his trademark grab-and-zip finish. The crowd always loved it and, yes, sometimes it zipped a bit too much, but he had to answer the rookie's shot. His swing was built on power and anger. He had the muscles that showed all of his hours of toil. With adrenaline and frustration pumping through his body, he transitioned to the downswing with all he had. The slight upslope he was on caused his transition to be off and his upper body fired early. The result was that he came into the ball a fraction steep. He corrected the best he could and the contact and finish looked normal to everyone else in the world.

However Cy, holding on to the ultimate tuning fork, knew immediately that he had a jumper on his hands and he started barking at the ball, "Sit!"

Steele's ball landed three feet past the hole and took a leap over the green into the primary rough. He was holding his finish, leaning forward, and screaming at the ball. Once his pleading had gone unanswered, he tore his club back down to the ground in a fit of anger. Turf flew everywhere. The announcers who loved the game and held its values in such high esteem were awkwardly silent as they knew that Cy brought in the big TV ratings that paid their salaries. His behavior had modeled that of a petulant youth his entire career. With the cameras off, they lamented his adolescent behavior but when on the air they could only offer platitudes.

Sitting up and to the right of the green in a palm tree, Big Mo had a huge smile on his face. Tom had turned a challenge into an opportunity and stayed in his flow state. He had processed the obstacle well and adapted his play. Mo was curious if Tom was ready to take the last two steps of having momentum always working in his favor.

The action on the thirteenth green took only twelve minutes to play out. However, to the people who were ensnared by the drama of this two-man battle, it was entire week's worth of intrigue. Cy had been unimpressed by his lie. He had scoffed at the ball mark and played as if he had been the victim of a heinous crime. He was setting the stage for a fantastic chip and he wanted to ensnare young Tom into feeling his advantage too greatly. With any luck the rookie might not be aggressive enough on his putt. He had made a few mighty practice swings and stared at his lie from multiple angles. In fact, he had drawn a break, as the ball was sitting with plenty of access to the back of the ball. This was all he needed to loft a shot high in the air, and once on the green the ball could roll softly past the flag to four or six feet. Executing under pressure was Steele's forte and with precision he lofted the ball up and had his uphill putt. But the fact that Tom made his putt ahead of Cy's miss was a study in contrast; Tom's effort was swift and clean, while Cy's was long and drawn out.

The two players moved the short twenty yards from the thirteenth green to the fourteenth tee and now it was Tom who had the honor and the one-shot advantage. He was five holes from winning the championship.

Both Foot and Mo knew what was lurking in the holes ahead and while Mo could only be summoned by the thought and actions of Tom himself, Foot had the conductor's wand and intended to lead to his fullest and help Tom get past the toughest of all beasts, the one that still lay ahead.

Between the fifteenth tee and the fairway sits a narrow but deep canyon that runs from right to left. Most players miss the canyon as a series of low coastal brush trees have grown in, and it looks as if you could walk across them. Deep at the bottom rests a creek bed and in a small and thorny crevice lives the final and most fearsome beast of Pebble Beach. Positioned perfectly to hear the players talk as they leave the tee, the Best of Self Doubt can not only hear what people say, but what they think. When a competitor combines the mistake of getting ahead of oneself with the hope of victory, often an inner voice of self-doubt rears its head and flies into the thoughts and muscles of its victim.

Hazards become larger, holes become smaller, and time stands still. Thoughts get fuzzier and muscles tighten, leading to rigid swings. Pebble Beach is the perfect playground for self-doubt as the final holes have hazards everywhere and the history of the past events makes any accomplishment appear more significant.

Tom and Cy managed solid pars on the long uphill dogleg right par-five fourteenth. The hole, like most at Pebble Beach, has plenty of subtle intrigue. The distance from tee to green is a long banana-shaped ascent up to the highest green on the golf course. The fairway slopes right to left and the hole plays left to right. The tee shot and the second shot are enough to challenge any golfer and would garner more attention if not for the drama that surrounds the green.

If you don't hit the fairway off the tee, you are left begging for distance on your second shot; and if you manage to hit the fairway, the layup is still no bargain. The ideal third for most is a 115-yard shot from the left half of the fairway, but the challenge is the pitch of the fairway, for any layup that comes in low up the hill with even a pinch of hook on it can easily find its way into the left rough. The player who overcompensates for the pitch and leaves it to the right is forced to play from the wrong side of the hole, aiming at a much smaller target with a more difficult landing angle and daunting spin issues.

Either way, the third shot is played to a downward facing kidney-shaped green that from the bird's eye view looks quite large by Pebble Beach standards. At ground level and in reality, the green is one of the smallest and hardest to hold on the course. The left side of the green is guarded by a massive bunker that captures all but the most well-struck shots, and the bailout to the right side of the green can often be worse as the surface is too pitched to hold any shots. Any ball that lands there will end up coming down to the front of the green and from there the player is too close to the hole and must take on either the edge of the bunker or risk going over the back of the green, which brings about a whole new set of challenges. The hole locations for the fourteenth green are in fact almost always on the left side, and therefore playing from the left and underneath the hole becomes critically important.

Both players had found the fairway with their drives, but while Tom played to the left center with his second, Cy had advanced his second almost too close to the hole and had his ball come to rest on the far left edge. Yet he survived a bothersome kick forward off the pitched fairway, and the advantage was to Cy for their third shots. Tom's ball carried well into the back of the green and checked up on the back edge of the green, a fraction of an inch from rolling down the closely mown section over the green—a near-disaster that would have led to an almost certain bogey. Cy nipped his gap wedge perfectly and left himself fifteen feet from above the hole and to the left. Tom putted to five feet short, having misread the speed of the green. Cy meanwhile had hit a spike mark with his attempt and then tapped in for par while letting off a little steam in the process. Tom, by this time being well aware of Cy's tactics, let the anger slide by him and focused on his ticklish par putt. His putt rolled true and fell in the top side of the hole for a par.

The final group and its entourage of cameras, media reporters, and officials moved another 25 feet up the hill to the fifteenth tee and for one of the few times all day had to wait to play. Tom and Foot had the tee but stood back and to the right to wait their turn. The wait didn't favor Tom and Cy knew it. Fifteen plays south to north and, while short in distance, comes with the extra pressure of having a tight out of bounds line along both sides of the hole. The right side OB in particular was very much in view from the tee. Tom's miss since turning pro had been a block to the right when he struggled to square up the club-face through impact. There were lots of causes, but regardless, the result had often been a round killer for him.

Now up one shot with four holes to play, the last thing he wanted to do was slow down his rhythm and especially on fifteen. His track record on the hole for the week had been spotty—two bogeys and a par that would have been a bogey if not for a fifteen-foot curler in round one. None of this information was available to Foot; he hadn't been following Tom throughout the week. Right now, Tom looked from the outside to be in a groove.

When the fairway cleared and Tom pulled his driver, the routine looked the same, as did the set-up. But the result was a high block fade that started right and had no chance of coming back. Tom's body language told the story to all watching as his right shoulder immediately leaned left and his entire torso leaned forward. His face showed the anguish of the miss.

CHAPTER 5

Fearless

When Tom's ball sailed OB, he knew was going to have to tee it again. Before he could do that, Steele jumped at his chance to add further pressure by taking the tee with strong body language and hammering a three-wood that split the fairway.

Cy's choice of club added further doubt to Tom's process, because clearly fifteen was a hole that could be played with driver or three-wood. Now hitting his third shot just seconds after his worst swing of the day, he needed to pick a club and stay committed to it.

Foot had watched the ball sail right and grimaced. He knew the Beast of Self Doubt was around, and he was also pretty sure, with fewer golfers on the course, that the other beasts would start showing up as well. Now his player needed to pick a club and hit it with conviction.

"Tom, driver is your play here, no doubt about it."

Tom looked at Foot and the caddy could see his player's face getting a little narrow.

"Tom, walk me through your target on this one."

Foot was doing all he could to get Tom to talk; talking at this moment was better than thinking.

"That's the problem, Foot," Tom said quietly. "I can't get a solid target that I can commit to."

Foot was ready with his answer.

"Fifteen yards right of the left tree line with a baby cut and it will run for days when it lands."

With the help of Foot, Tom laced a low drive that caught the downslope of the fairway and released. He had a ball in play, and he chased the ball down the fairway with a strong gait.

Foot kept up with Tom and knew he had some more work to do. The last four holes of a major championship typically don't favor a block fade. He also wanted to slow his player down. They might be waiting on every shot on the closing holes, and he had to help Tom adapt. Foot caught him right as he made it past the Beast of Self Doubt's home.

"Tom, let's slide over to the left side of the fairway here. I want to show you something about this green, and the angle is better from the left." Foot knew they had some extra time because Cy would be first to play, but he had to call out to his fast-walking player.

Tom looked back and realized he had left Foot in his dust in the commotion of the second tee shot finding the fairway. At least it had been a commotion for him. His brain had been all over the place as he addressed the ball. It was a miracle that he hadn't jacked the second ball OB, just like the first.

The pair moved to the left side of the fairway and just as Foot had thought, the green was full as was the sixteenth tee. It would be another few minutes before they would need to be ready to play their shot.

Foot started in with an odd but pointed question. "Tell me, Tom, how many other quirky misses do you carry around in your bad shot purse? It would be good to know about them now because the Beast of Self Doubt has an all-access pass to that satchel and it's not a fair fight if I don't know as much as he does."

Tom turned and while at first unsure of what Foot had said, immediately picked up Foot's point by seeing the caddy's frank expression. He, like all golfers, had a few misses that showed up from time to time. In fact, they often showed up at the wrong time. He had just never heard it explained in the manner in which Foot had chosen.

"I have a snap hook, a chunk, a skull, a toe, a heel, and my big one is the high right block," Tom said.

"Wow, you must get tired of carrying that purse around with you—it sounds pretty heavy."

Foot was on the edge with his player and he knew it. Tom had been hitting great shots and putting extremely well, but the last four holes would take almost an hour and that was more than enough time for his surroundings to engulf him. The miss off the tee would have rattled even a tour veteran and Foot needed to flush out where his player was mentally.

Tom responded. "Yes, most of them are from years ago and as I practice they fade in the background. Still, they are there and the block has cost me some cuts this year. It is really frustrating."

Foot was happy with the response and knew that he could unpack his next point off the sixteenth tee. Their dialogue had helped Tom and it was time to get to their ball.

The fifteenth green is similar to the thirteenth green, sloped back to front and right to left. The pitch on fifteen is softer and the green bigger. The best spot to play from is short and to the left; short iron shots can often be hit to very close range, because the winds coming off the ocean also can help hold up a properly played ball. Fifteen is a birdie hole and Cy Steele knew it.

His eight-iron approach from the downhill lie started fifteen feet left of the flag. The sound of contact told all educated ears that he had pured the shot. As the ball reached its apex it hit the wind perfectly, and like a pillow allowing a head to rest, the wind afforded the ball to land softly. Unfortunately for Cy, the downhill lie changed the loft on his club and his ball landed sixteen feet past the flag and didn't spin back. The firm turf grass conditions throughout the course remained one of the biggest obstacles for all competitors. Cy had done everything correctly and now had a downhill, left-to-right putt that could easily get away from him and he knew it. His reaction was a little more muted than earlier in the round, but his misfortune was accompanied by a series of hand gestures.

Tom's shot into fifteen was a full gap wedge that landed eight feet short right of the flag. It caught much more of the hill and his lie had been on a slight upslope. Unlike Cy's ball, Tom's took a high vertical bounce and had enough zip to start coming back down the slope. This worked against Tom as he was already below the hole and his ball ended up at the front of the green. Both players had hit crisp shots from the fairway and yet neither had a makeable putt.

Cy would have loved to make a birdie, but knew the real pressure was on Tom. Cy lagged his putt to three feet past the hole and marked his ball. Tom struck his putt firmly and on a good line and came up two feet short left. Both players found the cup with their second putts and Steele retook the lead by a shot.

The final group stood on the sixteenth tee and peered down the dogleg right par-four. The ocean shone in the distance. The championship hung in the balance. Cy had the comfortable position of having the honor and strode around the tee with authority. His physical presence was significant. He played a two-iron down the left side the fairway and had what looked to be a short iron into the green. Tom played a draw down the middle of the fairway and ended up closer to the hole than Cy.

Cy kept up his charge walking down the sixteenth fairway, while Tom and Foot walked some 40 yards behind. The dialogue started up again with Foot attempting to share with his young player how to get past the Beast of Self Doubt. "It looks like we did a good job of cutting a hole in that bad shot purse of yours, Tom. Your last three shots were struck with commitment."

"I am not sure they are all out of there," Tom replied. "I have been all over the place in my mind and somehow the ball is still going straight. That might not cut it over these last few holes, Tom. We need to keep feeding Mo with quality shots and combine that with a heart that is willing to fail completely. The question is, can you be fearless?"

Foot asked his question with great sincerity. He wanted to see if Tom was ready to take on this final challenge and he knew that all three beasts would be lurking in the trees to the left of the six-teenth green. Mo couldn't survive all these beasts if Tom didn't have a mindset of total commitment and being comfortable with failing for all to see.

"What do you mean by fearless?" Tom asked.

"I mean being ready to play the shots you know how to play and being comfortable with the fact that you may miss every one of those shots. You may crash and burn, you may lose the golf tournament, people may laugh at you. You may have all those things happen and you have to be good with that. That is being fearless, and the combination of quality shots and a fearless heart renders the beasts powerless."

"I can hit great shots," Tom said. "I also miss shots as well and have never been on this stage before. It is really hard to not get caught up in having all these people watching me play golf. Think of the status I will have if I can pull this off—I could be set for life."

"Yes," Foot said, "and between that dangerous thought and the embarrassment of falling flat on your face in these final three holes exists your opportunity. Seldom have I seen a person who chases status ever obtain enough. Status is like candy for the beasts, they can't get enough of it and it repels Mo. Staying shot to shot and loving the challenge of hitting great shots is what fuels Mo and repels the beasts."

Tom and Foot had covered the distance to their ball and eaten up the time they had to wait for the green to clear. It was Cy's turn to play, but his line of flight was over their ball so they stayed out to the right.

Tom turned to Foot. "I get it," he said, "we go for it. Each shot is an opportunity to execute and experience the feedback from the ball once struck."

Foot affirmed his words with a smile and offered.

"It is an amazing challenge, Tom, but you're up for it."

They walked over to Tom's ball as Cy's ball left his clubface. He had played a draw to the back left hole location. The sixteenth fairway runs downhill and right to left and the green sits well below the fairway. The ocean breezes come from directly behind the green, which is surrounded by a variety of trees. Some block the wind, some aren't dense enough to stop it. Cy's choice of a draw at the center of the green was the right choice. However, choosing correctly and executing can be two different things on a seaside links and his downhill lie combined with his trap draw action caused the ball to come out lower then desired. This did not afford the natural pillow of wind the opportunity to drop the ball in the middle of the green and release to the hole. Rather the ball came in low and hot, landed on the back third of the green, and pitched forward over the green into the primary rough. Cy's power was such an asset most weeks of the year, but in this championship his inability to control his swing speed with the irons had cost him dearly.

From the moment Steele's ball was in the air, Foot was giving Tom his numbers.

"It's 117 front, 139 hole. The downhill lie should make the ball come out lower than normal, which can impact how the wind affects the shot. I like a hold-off fade here so we keep the clubface from turning over. The line is middle of the green—you can let the slope of the green move the ball left for you."

Tom saw the gap wedge staring at him and knew right away it was the club for the shot. He locked in on his target, and came into his address position with the club in his right hand. His eyes left the target to set both hands on the club and place it square to the target. He then gave his target a final look and went into his swing. His knees, hips and then torso all adjusted for the downhill lie and the ball came off with solid contact.

The ball reached for every yard it could into the ocean breeze and landed almost halfway into the green.

The putting surface was turning a light brown, and right on cue the ball bounced forward and started breaking to the left. The grandstands that surround the green erupted with applause as the ball rolled closer and closer to the hole. It crescendoed as the ball came to rest two feet from the hole.

Foot handed Tom his putter and they exchanged a knowing glance. The beasts had been sitting in the trees to the left, just waiting for his mind to wander into what might be, what could be, and what it would mean. They were left wanting. Tom's mindset for a challenge and a fearless heart had quashed their power, and he had that magic tingle that comes when Big Mo is with you.

CHAPTER 6

Are you a Contagious Champion

Tom's birdie was assured on sixteen and that meant that Steele had to get up and down to stay tied. Few players in the world could match Cy's short game skills. However, all players that are over a green in tall grass benefit from access to the back of the ball, and Cy's lie was so bad that he had to mark it to make sure it was his. Once the ball was replaced exactly as before, the task of getting an uphill fifteen-foot putt was the primary job. Cy never played from out of position on a golf hole quickly. If he was going to make a bogey, he was going to take his time. He also knew that this would give Tom plenty of time to think about his tap-in and maybe get ahead of himself thinking about seventeen and eighteen.

Cy took several enormous practice swings to get a feel for the tension in the turf and to get a sense of where the ground was relative to his ball. All of this made for great viewing both live and on TV. It built up the moment and once his ball landed just on the green and bounded past the hole, it was clear to all that he really had no shot.

Cy took another several minutes to eventually miss his par putt and Tom then smoothly made his birdie. The match saw yet another two-shot swing and the action moved 50 yards west to the final two holes.

The seventeenth hole at Pebble Beach from the national championship tee measures 208 yards and plays directly towards the ocean.

The winds are a major factor and there are no trees or obstructions to block its path. The green has two distinct sections divided by a ridge that runs from front left to back right. The back left half of the green sits surrounded by sand and tall grass. The flagstick from this distance appears as a lone sentinel of safety amidst the peril.

Neither player had an answer for the tee shot, and both players found their balls bunkered. Steele's was short left in one of the largest bunkers on the course. Still, his ball was just 30 feet from the hole and, importantly, he was underneath the hole. Tom had played his one-iron and caught it flush. In fact, it was too flush and he caught a break when it went into the bunker over the green as a ball in the rough at seventeen is a much worse fate than the bunker. Tom was closer to the hole, but his downhill bunker shot was almost impossible to stop.

Cy was first to play and splashed out to five feet on the right side of the hole. Tom played smartly to the left of the flag and it released almost to the front of the green, which left him eighteen feet. The back-and-forth match continued to entertain the crowd.

Foot went over to Tom to clean his ball.

"Tom, this green has some grain in it that befuddles most players. We have drawn a break by having this putt. It looks like it breaks, but the grain keeps it straight. The trick is to hit it firm enough to hold the line. It's the challenge in front of you, and you can make this putt."

Tom surveyed the line from behind the ball, got locked into the spot on the hole where he wanted the ball to roll, and came into his address position. He left the spot with his eyes as he came to rest over the ball, but the picture of the spot remained in his mind and he rolled his ball. The ball climbed the hill and it made a sound as it chewed up the grass in its path. It rolled like on a razor's edge and, like a razor, it was straight. It rolled with purpose and it went right in the cup for a par.

Cy's world darkened, his putt had break in it and from what he had just seen he also had some pace issues to deal with.

His sidehill putt was actually more difficult than a straight downhill putt because he had to get the ball up the hill and then back down into the cup, all within five feet. One false roll and the ball would be four feet by. He steadied himself over his ball, took several practice strokes looking directly at the ball, and made a quality stroke. The ball left his club with purpose and climbed up to the right, but it didn't break down as much as he had planned. It stayed on the high side while it passed the cup. The crowd groaned. His comebacker for bogey was no picnic, but he coaxed it in the left side of the hole, and the twosome moved to the final hole.

Steele was weathered and mad. He had fought his hardest to stay with the kid. He just couldn't gain control over the group, which was his main weapon. His golf was excellent, but his mind had been prepared to be in front after six holes. The only thing that could save him now was if the kid had a train wreck on the final hole. This wasn't impossible.

The eighteenth at Pebble Beach is one of the all-time risk-reward holes in golf.

The Pacific Ocean sits to the left and the mansions line up on the right. In between, a thin slice of grass grows with several bunkers to the right off the tee. It finishes with a 100-yard long bunker that hugs a rock wall along the ocean's edge. At 535 yards long, it is the type of par-five that can yield a three or extract an eight without much difficulty.

Tom and Cy stepped to the tee and waited for the group in front to clear. The waves were coming in with regularity and the setting was magnificent. While waiting, Foot could tell that Cy was looking to attempt another Machiavellian move. He thought about blocking its path and considered his options. He decided that if Tom was going to reach the heights that he saw in him, it was best to let him handle it on his own.

Cy slowly bounced his ball off the face of his driver, the sound tinny and frequent. The act itself was quite challenging and was yet another example of his exceptional hand-eye coordination. He ended the routine and grabbed the ball in his hand when he could tell it was close to Tom's turn to hit.

"You know, Tom, that rock wall on the left cost almost six million dollars to make. The winnings from this huge event would only cover a sixth of that. Can you believe how much money this place must rake in to be able to afford a six-million dollar wall?"

Tom turned to Cy with indifference. "That's impressive, Cy. I wonder what it cost to buy one of those homes sitting out of bounds on the right? My guess is they are running almost ten million. The good news is that the fairway is nice and wide, and at least this week we don't have to pay to walk on it."

And with that Tom aimed out over the ocean and hit a high fade that landed just past the second tree that grows in the fairway. Foot leaned back while holding onto the bag and gave himself a moment to breathe in as the ball started to fade back to safety. The kid had accepted the poison, redirected it, and actually thrown it back in Cy's direction. Most importantly he had ended his talk on his target.

Cy took a different line up the right side and clipped the first tree in the fairway. He watched in dismay as his ball ricocheted right into the bunker. His misery trap was now a party of one and he skulked his way up the fairway with his Open chances coming to an end.

As Tom arrived at his ball, Cy had already played up the right side of the fairway and there was Foot with his familiar refrain.

"You've got 223 front, 245 hole, with a slight helping breeze coming out of the left. The front of the green is firm and should reward a well-hit shot. Play away, Tom."

The bag tilted and Tom saw his one-iron gleaming at him. He knew his favorite shot was a cut one-iron. With the eyes of the world watching, and a two-shot lead in the balance, Tom aimed at the left greenside bunker and swung with freedom. The contact was thin and the ball started out further left than either Tom or Foot would have wanted, but as the ball reached its peak a brief breeze kicked up and pushed the ball to the right just enough for it to come back into play and land over the bunker. It bounded up through the apron and onto the front edge of the green.

Tom exhaled and Foot looked skyward with his eyes and a gesture of thanks with his hand. The announcers caught it and thought he was having a spiritual moment, but Foot was giving a nod to his old friend Mo. He had shown up once again to help one of his players reach a new level of accomplishment. This one had been special and now Foot was going to be on the bag for an Open champion. Even for Foot, life was full of surprises.

Cy had one final shot to play and didn't let the opportunity pass as he flagged a low one-hop-and-stop nine-iron to six feet and let the crowd's roar fill his tanks. His next major would be in less than a month at St. Andrews, and he would be back.

The applause as they walked up was fantastic and Steele, for all his faults, knew when the world was watching and let Tom take his walk up to the green by himself. Foot also stayed back a bit and was able to take in the setting of Pebble Beach with the grandstands full and all the flags ripping atop the lodge. He settled near the front of the green and looked at Tom's putt. He knew this break like he knew them all.

"We've got 32 feet here, Tom. Play it a cup out on the right with no trick speeds and let her rip!" It was his final charge for Tom and he stepped back and held the flagstick. Tom went into his routine, and Foot allowed himself a momentary forward-looking action.

He started unscrewing the flag from the stick and got in position to grant himself the caddy's trophy, which is the flag from the eighteenth hole.

Tom was locked in on the target, came to rest over the ball, and had rolled his ball with purpose within eight seconds. The ball never left its line and as it fell in the cup for an eagle three, Tom raised his putter and soaked in the adoration of the golfing world. He was the U.S. Open champion. He turned to Foot as he pulled his ball out of the cup and bear hugged his frail giant of a caddy. The emotions came out of him, and the two embraced like they had been friends for life.

Once the crowd quieted down, Cy milked the stage for all its worth and rolled in the four of his own. His round of 70 would have been good enough to win each of the last eight Opens and his legacy was still intact. The rookie had caught lightning in a bottle.

Mo, who had been sitting just above the large white scoreboard to the left of eighteen, quietly drifted back to his cave. His slight assist on Tom's second shot had been just a nudge and the wind was helping anyway. He wasn't sure what kind of champion Tom would end up being and if he would learn the final lesson of developing a personal way to build momentum that he could share with others. However, he was certainly attracted to this player and had high hopes for his future.

The trophy presentation and press conference were a blur for Tom. He answered each question as directly as he could. Most of the reporters wanted to know how he had come out of nowhere. What was the difference? His answers seemed a little odd to many, but to those people who had been around Foot over the years they knew he had worked his magic. Tom kept saying, "We made a plan, got ready for an adventure, and then saw our shots and took them. All of a sudden Mo showed up, and before I knew it the day was over. It was one of the fastest rounds of golf I've ever played."

In truth the round was just like every other final round of the Open, but Tom's experience had been so different than his other rounds that it felt much shorter. Finally, the madness was over and Tom said goodbye to his college friends and called his caddy Billy to make sure he was okay. All Tom really wanted to do was find Foot and go down to the rock wall on eighteen with the trophy and celebrate. Foot had been accepting pats on the back from his peers as he waited for Tom to finish his interview. He saw the trophy first and then the tired smile of Tom.

"What do you say we get these clubs in your car and find our way down to the eighteen green to see if we can get Mo to show up and celebrate with us?" Foot offered.

"You read my mind, Foot," came the reply, and within 15 minutes they were on the rock wall with their feet hanging over it, the trophy between them in the bunker.

Pebble Beach at sunset can range from off the charts stunning to cold, foggy and damp. On this evening it was somewhere in the middle—just a few clouds, 56 degrees, and with small waves lapping up against the rocks. Tom started to let the events of the day sink in and their conversation turned to some of the shots he had hit.

"You know, Foot, there wasn't a single shot I hit today that I haven't hit before. All those shots were in me from all of my practice and preparation. How is it that today I strung them all together?"

Foot had hoped their conversation would get to this matter.

"Tom, I have spent my life helping people enjoy this special place. My job as a caddy is to help them unlock their best golf while playing this legendary track. As a professional golfer, you had a huge advantage over my regular loops because the execution part of the game is really quite difficult. For the 13-handicap recovering from a bad shot is hard, and for the 25-handicap it is almost impossible. They wear their bad shots like tattoos. You had the extra challenge of the pressure and the status that comes with trying to perform on the U.S. Open stage. However, you and that bogey golfer have a lot in common when it comes to momentum. It is really important how you react to your poor shots. On fifteen today you could have really faded, and I am guessing something like that has derailed you in the past."

"That conversation we had on fifteen was big," Tom interjected.

"Exactly," Foot said.

"You chose to stay focused on a quality shot for your next shot."

"Yes, but how did they all string together?"

Foot continued, "We had a routine, we had a mindset for adventure, and you were able to picture the shot you wanted to take before you pulled the club. My job as your caddy was to help get you locked in as we came to each shot, to help you prep for your next shot and regardless whether it was good or bad to not wear your last shot for too long. That is when Mo shows up and helps you reach new heights."

"The question, Mr. U.S. Open Champion, is now that you understand this, are you going to share it with others or keep it to yourself? It is your move."

For the first time in a while, Foot really stared at Tom with purpose. He was dead serious. Tom looked at Foot, looked at the trophy sitting between them and looked out at the ocean.

Finally he turned and said, "Foot, how do I not share it, as you shared it with me today and we had never met before? I don't feel like I own this feeling or this process. But without sounding like an idiot, how do I share a spirit or a feeling?"

Mo, who had been circling for a while, decided this was his cue and swept down to sit on a rock just beneath Foot and Tom. His entrance was a bit of a shock to Tom, who didn't think Mo was actually real. Foot leaned over and held Tom from falling backwards into the bunker.

"I guess I should take the lead on this one, Foot," Mo said.

"Tom, you share momentum with others by your body language, movements and words. People who do this are rewarded by having great relationships with others and often fantastic experiences in life and sport."

"Seeking Mo allows two people to work with each other even while they are competing. Golf has many examples of where players can work off each other's good shots to propel both of them to a new level of accomplishment."

Tom was soaking it all in. He had been through a lot and thought his day had essentially ended with the eagle on eighteen. This was so much more.

"Okay, this makes sense, but can I have some baby steps to take first? Foot has been practicing this for years."

Mo gave a nod to Foot who shared.

"It comes down to three things: be contagious, be an encourager, and be a mentor."

"Every interaction you have with others is a chance to pass on your positive energy. This is the definition of contagious. When you come to a challenge yourself or with others, harness your spirit for adventure and use encouraging words. Finally as the first few steps start to become normal habits for you, more and more people will seek to be around you and at that point you can pass on what we are talking about here. That is mentoring."

Mo added, "It's not just on the golf course, Tom, it's every day of your life. And as you will now see as a major championship winner, the challenges will present themselves again and again. Find a group of like-minded friends and enjoy the adventure."

With that, Mo lifted himself into the air and was gone amidst the darkening sky. Foot and Tom gathered their things, raked their way out of the bunker, and walked back onto the eighteenth fairway. They were two friends who had shared an amazing day together, one was about to face the rigors of playing like a major champion in the future and the other in a week or so would look to help another golfer uncover their own way to finding Big Mo.

PEBBLE BEACH GOLF LINKS

Beast of Headlines

Mo's Cave

Beast of Self Doubt

Beast of Expectation

Printed in Great Britain
by Amazon

43794178R00059